You Got This!
Mama

by
Megan Park

Illustrated by
Sania Zahid

sugar.bean.PUBLISHING

You Got This, Mama!

Written by Megan G. Park

Illustrated by Sania Zahid

ISBN: 978-1-7363303-1-9 (paperback)
ISBN: 978-1-7363303-2-6 (hardback)

Printed in the United States of America.

First printing, 2020.

sugar.bean.PUBLISHING

♡ Dedication ♡

This book is dedicated to:

All the Mamas out there,
no matter what stage of "Momming" you are in.
You are everything.

The two boys
The source of all my wrinkles and smiles, who call me
Mama and are doing a remarkable job
raising me.

My Mama
the best human to ever live.

The moment you laid eyes on that sweet face,
The face that made you mom in the first place,

Your whole world changed as you kissed that fresh head. You waited a while.

"I got this!"

you said.

Baby girl   5lbs
27-12-2020

Tired?

Yes. But never this
happy before.
Snuggles on chest,
belly laughs
till you're sore.

With smiles so **big**,
they take up your whole face,
Tub splashes, grass stains,
hide and seek,
and chase.

Momming is fun!
The best thing you have done.
"I got this!"
you shout as you
smile and run.

But on days when momming
is sometimes too **hard,**
Your bucket is empty,
Your **spirit** is marred,

You no longer "got this," unsure what to do,

Your title of "Mom" didn't come with a clue.

Then those **small,** sticky fingers grab hold of your hand.

And those sweet,
little lips share a kiss not yet planned.

Your heart is reminded that the days sure are **long,** But years will fly by seemingly quick as a **song.**

For momming was meant to be tough, you see.

Nothing worth **cherishing** comes easily.

When home is a **mess**, and the
house a disaster,
Remember to turn to our
All-Knowing Master.

"You got this!"
says God.
"Cause when you don't, I do.
We got this together;
they're my children too.

I chose them **special**;
they were meant for your heart.
You mom oh so well,
always have from the start."

"You sing, you laugh, you tickle, you cheer."

"You watch, you pray, you worry, you fear."

"You got this!

No doubt. You are
fit for the role.

Without you, this
family would not be
whole."

"For mommies are teachers, leaders, and friends,
Coaches, chauffeurs, chefs...
the job never ends."

One last **peek**,
one more tuck,
'cause that's just what we do.
Sacrifice our own comforts,
without a
"thank you."

So when momming gets **hard**,
you just call on His name,

Tell yourself,
"I got this!"
and get back in the game.

Your little ones are constantly looking to you.
They see **more** than you know,
they feel **all** that you do.

To them, you are **queen**,
their mommy, and their **rock**.
Just doing your **best**,
is the key in the **lock**.

So, think back on the days and moments of bliss.
And Mom, tell yourself one more time,

"I got this!"

ABOUT THE AUTHOR

Megan Park is Mama to 2 young, energetic boys, from whom she receives daily inspiration, unconditional love, and gray hairs. She is a working mom in and out of the home, with goals and ambitions, and a knack for organization. From a young age, she discovered her love of writing and poetry, and has written hundreds of poems and stories over the years. She received her Bachelor's degree in Sociology from Brigham Young University, and is happily married to her high school sweetheart. With a passion for celebrating diversity, it's an important theme that can be seen throughout all of her work. She loves sushi, true-crime documentaries, and singing loudly. She finds purpose and joy in motherhood, creating, and operating two online businesses. You Got This Mama is her first book.

ABOUT THE ILLUSTRATOR

Sania Zahid is an Illustrator from Pakistan who loves to play with colors. Since childhood she was influenced by arts & designs and wanted to pursue her passion in this field. She received her Bachelor's degree in Graphics Designing in 2015 & has since worked as an illustrator for the gaming industry & children's media. She tries her best to bring positive change in society by using her superpower i.e. her Art. She also loves to create fun & whimsical art for children, which is not just limited to books. She is an avid gamer and currently designing multiple artwork for games as well. Her aim is to incorporate diversity and positivity in all her work. She hopes her artwork drives the audience's attention away from everyday stress and provides a moment to appreciate the innocent beauty around us.

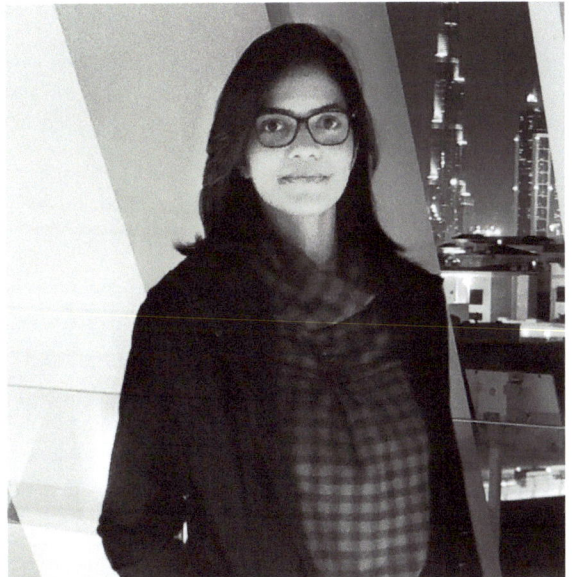

www.ingramcontent.com/pod-product-compliance
Lightning Source LLC
Chambersburg PA
CBHW041553040426
42447CB00002B/166